DATE			

DEATH IS NATURAL

DEATH IS NATURAL

by Laurence Pringle

Four Winds Press   New York

The author wishes to thank Dr. Donn E. Rosen, Curator,
Department of Ichthyology, The American Museum of
Natural History, for reading and suggesting changes
in the manuscript of this book.

Photo credits

Bureau of Sport Fisheries and Wildlife, photo by E. R. Kalmbach, p. 18.
F.A.O. Photo, p. 25.   Michigan Department of Conservation, p. 23.
South African Tourist Corporation, p. 45.
All other photographs are by the author.

LIBRARY OF CONGRESS CATALOGING IN PUBLICATION DATA

Pringle, Laurence P.
  Death is natural.

  Bibliography: p.
  Includes index.
  SUMMARY: A simple discussion of death as it applies to
  the plant and animal kingdom.
  1. Death (Biology)—Juvenile literature. [1. Death] I. Title.
QH530.P74   574.2   76-48923
ISBN 0-590-07440-7

Published by Four Winds Press
A Division of Scholastic Magazines, Inc.,
New York, N.Y.
Copyright © 1977 by Laurence Pringle

Printed in the United States of America

Library of Congress Catalog Card Number: 76-48923

1 2 3 4 5   81 80 79 78 77

In memory of Mr. Big,
Kahlua,
and Purr-vert,
cat-friends
who died too young.

Contents

～ About This Book ～

～ Death is a natural part of life. Sooner or later, every living thing dies. We know this, but we usually don't think about death very much. Then, a pet dog or cat may be killed. A friend or a member of your own family dies. Suddenly death seems very close, and frightening.

So far as we know, humans are the only animals that remember, in any detail, a dead individual. We are also the only animal that is able to think ahead to the end of life. Death has special meanings for us. It may bring sadness and change to our lives.

It also brings questions: What happens to a living thing after it dies? How does the death of one animal or plant affect others of its kind? Is death always a bad thing or can it have good effects?

In this book you will find some answers to these questions. You will read about a variety of living things, from little chipmunks and seedling plants to great whales and dinosaurs. Of course, they all die. By learning about the deaths of many kinds of living things, we may accept more easily this natural and necessary part of the history of each living thing.

The Travels of Atoms

A cottontail rabbit left the shelter of some weeds and hopped onto the road. The night was cool, and the pavement, still warm from spring sunshine, felt good underfoot. Suddenly, two bright lights shone on the rabbit. It hesitated, then ran. Too late. THUMP. The car drove on, and the rabbit lay still at the edge of the road.

The rabbit's brain was damaged, and had stopped working. It no longer sent or received messages from the animal's eyes and ears. The rabbit could not see or hear. Its brain also stopped sending and receiving messages from its muscles and organs. The rabbit could not move. Its heart had stopped beating. It did not breathe.

Blood stopped flowing through the rabbit's arteries and veins. No more food or oxygen reached the cells which made up the rabbit's body. The cells died by the million, like tiny fires winking out. Soon the rabbit's body was as cool as the night air. It had died.

We don't see much death, but it is there, all around us. Each day billions of insects die. Thousands of birds fly down to the ground, and never rise again. And cars kill hundreds of rabbits.

Before dawn, an opossum found the rabbit, dragged it into a field, and fed on it. Later that day a crow ate more of the rabbit. Bit by bit, the dead rabbit was being eaten by scavengers—animals which feed on dead animals or plants. The rabbit's body was not going to waste. Dead animals and plants never go to waste.

Other, microscopic organisms such as one-celled bacteria, fungi, and protozoa, were also "nibbling" away at the rabbit. Some of them had been within the rabbit's body before it died. Some had settled on the rabbit's body from out of the air. Some came from the soil.

These tiny organisms are almost everywhere on earth. They are called decomposers. They set to work when life ends. Decomposers break down, or decay, the remains of once-living things.

All life, from huge whales to microscopic bacteria, is made up of 30 or more elements. Some of the most abundant elements are carbon, hydrogen, oxygen, nitrogen, sulphur, calcium, and iron. Elements like these, in varying amounts, make up all plants and animals. They also make up soils, water, air, rocks, and other nonliving things.

Each element is made up of just one kind of atom. An atom can exist by itself, but it usually forms groups with other atoms. The groups are called molecules. Bacteria are able to break down big molecules into smaller molecules, and these molecules into atoms. This was happening within the muscles, organs, tissues, skin, and hair of the dead rabbit.

Energy is released when molecules are broken apart and rearranged. Food energy from the rabbit's molecules was used by bacteria, as well as by the opossum, and the crow.

Part of the rabbit's body touched the soil, and that part de-

cayed quickly. It was moist and dark there, just right for bacteria and other decomposers. They multiplied rapidly. Bacteria that died became food for other bacteria.

Within a few weeks the rabbit seemed to have vanished. Only a few bones, teeth, and tufts of hair were left. In time they would decay, too. Most of the rabbit had disappeared, but not a single atom of its body had been lost.

Some atoms were in the soil. Some were in the air. And many were already part of some living thing. The crow and the opossum contained some of the rabbit's atoms.

Nearly all of the rabbit's atoms were off on journeys. In the soil, some of its carbon atoms had joined with oxygen atoms to form molecules of carbon dioxide. The molecules were taken into the root of a wild raspberry bush that grew in the field. They were carried upward, from cell to cell, from the plant's roots to a leaf. There the atoms were rearranged and combined with hydrogen atoms. Molecules of sugar formed. They flowed through the plant's cells to some ripening berries.

A few days later, a boy rode his bicycle along the road and saw the raspberries. He stopped, dashed into the field, and ate

the delicious fruit. Then he noticed some bones beneath the bush. They were weathered and white. The boy decided to take the rabbit's skull home, as a kind of souvenir. He did not know that other souvenirs of the rabbit rode home within his body—some of the rabbit's atoms were in the berries he had eaten.

Most of the elements that make up your body come from food you have eaten, liquids you have drunk, or air you have breathed. Before reaching you, the atoms have been recycling. They have moved from living things to nonliving things, on and on, for millions of years. Their travels through time are a mystery. Many of the atoms may have been locked up in rocks for long periods of time. Some have been miles deep in the ocean, or high in the atmosphere.

Some of your atoms were definitely part of other living things. It is easy to trace them back a little ways. Just think of food you ate recently—perhaps chicken, lettuce, apple, fish. But where were these atoms a year ago—or millions of years ago? Atoms within your body may have once been part of a blade of grass, an octopus, a dinosaur, or even another person.

In a sense, we merely borrow a supply of the earth's ele-

ments for a while. We have to give them back. All living things give these elements back when they die and decay.

Although many people do not like to think about death and decay, others accept it as a fact of life. Before dying, some people ask that their bodies be burned (cremated) and their ashes scattered in a favorite forest or other wild place. It pleases them to think that their atoms might become part of a wildflower, tree, or songbird.

Although human bodies decay after death, some people believe that there is a soul, or spirit, that lives on afterward. In ancient Egypt, the bodies of dead kings were carefully preserved because people believed that this kept the souls of the kings alive. Usually, however, people believe that the soul leaves the body, and has an afterlife. According to different beliefs, the soul may go to a place of reward or punishment, to the sun, to a newborn baby, or to some other living thing, such as a tree or elephant.

The afterlife of a soul is often imagined to be happy, free of all the troubles most people have in their daily lives. So, many people have mixed feelings about the death of someone close to them. They are sad because the person has died, but are also pleased because they believe that the person's soul has gone on to its afterlife.

Some people believe there is no life after death. An afterlife is not the sort of idea that scientists can prove or disprove. However, scientists do agree on two facts about death. First, it is inevitable. Death is the natural end to all life.

Second, death is necessary. Without death and decay, many

atoms would be "locked up" in plants and animals. They could not be used by new living things. Think of the leaves that fall from trees, for example. Nearly two tons of this dead material falls onto an acre of forest floor each year. The life of a forest would be choked off if these leaves kept piling up, year after year. Fortunately, they decay. Their atoms are recycled to many living things, including the trees from which they fell.

Without death and decay, most recycling of the earth's vital elements would stop. It would not halt completely, because atoms are moved about and rearranged by blowing winds and flowing waters. But life as we know it would be impossible without death.

Death is an end, but it is also a beginning, for it is a necessary part of the continual recycling of the earth's elements.

Adding and Subtracting

When a city family moved to an old farm in the country, one of the first things they did was put up "No Hunting" signs. They wanted to increase the numbers of songbirds, rabbits, squirrels, woodchucks, and other wildlife. Their farm was to be like a Garden of Eden, with beautiful wild creatures all around.

But they were disappointed. As the years passed, the numbers of wild animals stayed about the same, and with good reason: the environment of their farm stayed about the same. It had only enough hiding places, nesting places, food, and other resources to support a certain number of animals year round. Each spring and summer many young animals were born, and

the wildlife population grew. By late fall, however, the numbers were dwindling fast. By the following spring the wildlife population was back where it had started.

The family hardly ever saw an animal die, but death was all around them. Most of the young birds and mammals died within a few months of birth. They died in nests because of cold and wet weather. They died of diseases. They were killed by accidents, and by foxes, owls, and other meat-eating animals (predators).

Their deaths were natural and necessary. All populations of animals and plants have a tremendous capacity for growth. A female cottontail rabbit may produce twenty young in a year. If all of these little rabbits survived to mate and produce litters of their own, a farm would soon be overrun with cottontails.

This does not happen. The numbers of rabbits and other wild animals stay about the same from year to year unless the living conditions change. Suppose a flood or other disaster strikes. Nearly all of the rabbits are wiped out. Then the environment gradually returns to normal, with the amount of food, hiding places, and other resources it had before. The rabbit

population returns to normal, too, as young are born, and other rabbits immigrate from surrounding areas.

An abundance of food and other resources seems to be a signal for some animals to produce more young. Biologists in Texas found this to be true of coyotes. In one part of the state coyotes were plentiful. They were using all of the available food, space, and other resources. In this area the female coyotes usually had four or five pups a year.

In another part of Texas, the coyote population was kept low by hunting, trapping, and poisoning. There was plenty of food and space available for more coyotes. In this area the female coyotes had about seven pups each year.

Plants also have a great capacity for increasing their numbers. Just one dandelion flower may produce seeds for more than a hundred new plants. Thousands of winged seeds spin down from a single maple tree. Each seed is capable of becoming a big tree. But there aren't enough resources—sunlight, water, minerals, space—to go around. Of all the seedlings that begin to grow, perhaps only one will reach full size. It replaces the parent tree when the old maple dies, and the maple tree population stays the same.

A gardener sometimes has to "thin" (pull out) some young vegetables so that others have space in which to reach full size. Often more than half of the seedling plants are tossed aside to die. "Thinning" also occurs naturally in populations of wild plants and animals. When some die, others are able to develop more fully and produce future generations.

Sometimes an animal population increases until it begins to destroy the very resources upon which it depends. This sometimes happens among large plant-eating mammals, such as deer. In many areas there are no more wolves or other predators of deer. Diseases, accidents, and hunting are not enough to keep deer numbers in check. The deer population grows and grows.

Eventually the deer begin to damage the shrubs and other plants upon which they feed. There is not enough good food to go around. The deer become sickly and produce fewer young. Their population levels off, but the deer are not healthy.

One remedy might be to bring in a population of wolves or other predators. Another might be to allow hunters to kill more deer. And another is to "let nature take its course." A

disease may eventually sweep through the population. An especially cold and snowy winter may cause many deer to starve. One way or another, the deer population may be reduced, at least for a few years. The plant life has a chance to recover, and the surviving deer are well fed and healthy. Once again, the well-being of the population depends on the death of many individuals.

For many thousands of years, the human population grew

slowly, if at all. People knew very little about diseases. They died of illnesses that we no longer need worry about. Getting enough food was another problem that often threatened human survival. Parents had many babies so that one or two would survive to be adults. For a long time the human population was like a population of rabbits or deer that was kept in check by disease, a limited food supply, and other factors in the environment.

Human numbers have increased as people learned how to grow more food, such as the wheat shown on the next page. They increased even faster as we learned how to prevent or cure many diseases. Babies now have much better chances of growing to be adults, and adults can expect to live longer lives. But millions of parents around the world still choose to have many babies. Most of them survive, so the earth's population keeps growing. It passed four billion in 1975 and may reach seven billion by the year 2000.

The human population is like a deer population which no longer has wolves or other animals preying upon it. Disease is no longer the fierce "predator" of people it once was. A lack of

food usually stops the growth of a deer population. The same may happen to people.

So far, the world's food supply has increased along with the numbers of people, although many people are poorly fed. Some starve to death. Many more will starve unless the population stops growing. The earth is like a farm. It is limited in size, resources, and in the amount of food it can produce.

This means that sometime, sooner or later, the human population must level off. Fortunately, we can choose how to stop our numbers from rising. Death by starvation is one way. Deciding to have fewer children is another. Deer, rabbits, and all other animals and plants do not have a choice. They usually produce many more young than their environments will support. The well-being of their populations depends on large numbers of their young dying early.

⤳ Death Brings Change ⤳

⤳ A young boy shrieked when he saw his cat walking across the lawn. The cat had a chipmunk in its mouth. He chased the cat and made it drop its prey, but he was too late. The chipmunk was dead.

The boy thought the cat was mean and vicious. But life is not that simple. Neither is death.

The cat was not being mean. It was simply being a cat, and cats of all kinds are hunters. To hunt — to stalk, attack, and kill prey — is a basic part of cat behavior. It has enabled cats to get food and survive for millions of years.

Although cats must learn to be skillful killers, hunting behavior is a characteristic that is passed from parent cats to their young, from one generation to the next.

This characteristic and others are part of a cat's genes, which are molecules or groups of molecules that are in all of the cells of each animal and plant. Sex cells also have these molecules. When two cats mate, a male sex cell (sperm) joins with a female sex cell (egg). We then say that the egg is fertilized. When this happens the genes of both parents are combined. They are like a set of chemical directions which determine what the fertilized egg will become.

Of course in this case it becomes a cat. But what sort of cat? Depending on the genes it gets from its parents, a fertilized egg might develop into a male or female cat. It might be a short-haired cat, or a long-haired cat. One thing is certain: it will have an urge to hunt.

Which brings us back to chipmunks. At first glance you may think that all chipmunks are alike. They certainly *look* much more alike than pet cats do. However, each one is unique in some ways. This may seem like a strange idea. We can tell at a glance that cats, and people, vary a lot, in their size, shape, color, and many other ways. It may come as a surprise that there is also great variety in other living things, including chipmunks, barnacles, trees, swans, and mosquitoes. Each individual is unique because it has a unique combination of genes.

Whenever animals or plants produce a new generation, genes are combined in new ways. This can lead to change, not just in individual organisms but in entire populations or species. For example, the color pattern on the fur of a chipmunk population might change. A change like this usually occurs after many, many generations and perhaps thousands of years. This change is called evolution.

Biologists in laboratories have studied ways in which evolution can occur. For example, by choosing certain mice and allowing them to mate, biologists can accurately predict what color fur will grow on the baby mice. They can also predict the eye color of fruit flies that hatch from eggs, simply by knowing the eye color of the parent flies. Laboratory studies like these help explain a lot of the variety and change that we see in nature.

Reproduction is the key to evolution. Among the chipmunks that do reproduce, for example, some have more young than others. Their young make up a greater share of the next generation. So the chipmunks that have the most young have the greatest chance of affecting the characteristics of future generations.

Of course, if an individual animal or plant does not reproduce, it has no effect on future generations. Suppose a chipmunk or lion or redwood tree is remarkably strong and healthy. This is fine for the individual animal or plant. But the population only benefits when the chipmunk, lion, or tree reproduces, and passes its characteristics on to the next generation.

So the ability to reproduce is important. So is the *opportu-*

nity to reproduce. This is where death comes in. Many animals and plants die before they can reproduce.

Often the ones that die are less fit in some way. Occasionally, for example, an albino chipmunk is born. An albino is an animal that lacks normal color in its skin, fur, or feathers, and also in its eyes. Albinos do not see very well. For this reason alone, an albino chipmunk might not live long. Also it would be very noticeable to foxes, owls, and cats. An albino chipmunk would probably be killed early in its life, before it mated and had young. Its opportunity to pass characteristics on to the next generation would also die.

Like chipmunks, all other living things have changed over the millions of years since life began. Populations of people are affected by most of the same factors that affect chipmunks. Because of their size and intelligence, of course, humans have never had much to fear from predatory animals. The main danger to human life has been, and still is, disease. That danger is much less now, thanks to better living conditions and medicines.

As a result, some people who might have been "weeded out" by an early death in the past are now able to live fairly normal lives. They may marry and have children. Their genes remain in their population. No one knows what effect this will have on the characteristics of human populations in the future. Time will tell, and so will a better understanding of death and change in all living things.

﹏ Species Die, Too ﹏

﹏ By studying the births and deaths of a population, you can sometimes tell a great deal about its future. If the number of young born are about the same as the number of individuals that die, the population will stay about the same. If births far outnumber the deaths, the population is growing fast. This is true of human populations in Mexico, India, and many African and Asian nations. Children and young adults make up a large part of these populations. They are likely to live long enough to produce young of their own, and add further to population growth.

Quite the opposite is true of some animal and plant populations. In these populations, most of the individuals are old and no longer produce young. Or deaths may outnumber births. In either case, this means that the population is not reproducing itself. It may die out completely. When all of the individuals and populations of a species die out, we call the species "extinct."

The extinction of a whole species is as natural as the death of an individual animal or plant. A tree dies, a dog dies, a flea dies, a person dies—we may not notice or we may grieve, but we accept death as inevitable. Extinction is also part of life, although a species may live for millions of years.

You can probably name some species or entire groups of species that are extinct—dinosaurs, dodos, saber-toothed cats, passenger pigeons. Besides these well-known examples, millions of other kinds of animals and plants have become extinct. Many are known only by fossils they left behind.

When a species becomes extinct, people sometimes say that it "failed," or that it wasn't "successful." It is rather foolish for humans to call dinosaurs or some other extinct group a failure. Dinosaurs existed for more than a hundred million years, while humans have so far lived for about four million. Judging

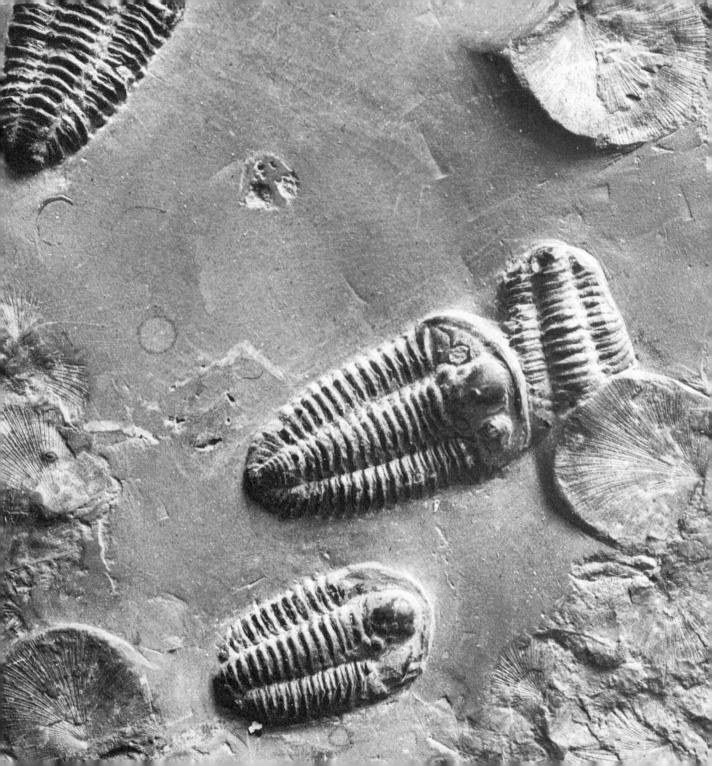

by their long existence, the dinosaurs were a tremendous success. Then they came to a natural end. So did the trilobites and brachiopods whose fossils are shown at the left.

Species usually become extinct when their environment changes. Perhaps the climate turns from warm to cold. Or a new kind of organism begins to compete for the resources of the environment.

If changes like these are gradual, a species may be able to adjust and survive. This is possible because of the variety of characteristics in the species. Suppose, for example, that a species of mouse is faced with a change in climate in the land where it lives. The climate grows colder and colder. If all of the mice were exactly alike, the species might be wiped out.

But the mice are not all alike. Some may have longer fur or some other characteristic that enables them to withstand the cold better than others. They reproduce, and pass this advantage on to other mice. Given enough time, the species may evolve in a way that allows it to survive in a colder climate.

Of course, many kinds of animals and plants have not been able to adapt to changing conditions and are now extinct. According to evidence from fossils, changes in climate may have

caused some extinctions in the past. But some extinctions are now being caused by people.

Humans had rather small effects on the earth's environment at first. But their intelligence, use of tools, and growing numbers have had great effects on other living things. People may have first reached North America about 11,000 years ago. Not long after, several species of large mammals, including mastodons, ground sloths, and camels, became extinct. They may have died out because of overhunting.

Since then the pace of extinction has quickened, and shows no sign of letting up. Worldwide, thousands of species of living things have died out. Many more are in danger of extinction.

This is perfectly natural. One species (humans) is increasing its numbers and trying to meet its needs by changing the environment. Other species die out as a result. This sort of thing has always gone on. However, it has never happened on this scale, with so many species becoming extinct in such a short time.

These extinctions are unusual in another way. For the first time, the main cause of extinction — the human species — is able to see and understand the full effects of its actions. People are intelligent enough to see that extinction of other living things is a loss to them, and perhaps a danger to their own existence.

Many people fear that tigers, elephants, and many other animals may soon exist only in zoos, not in the wild. They are alarmed at the thought of forests without wolves, skies without eagles, and oceans without whales. But these feelings are not shared by everyone. The survival of the cheetah in Africa may

not seem very important to a man there who is barely able to get enough food for his family.

Cheetahs and tigers are beautiful and unique, and that may be reason enough for people to try to save them from extinction. To scientists, however, the value of these creatures is more than physical beauty. These mammals and all other living things on earth are part of nature. They fit together with other organisms, like parts of a giant and intricate puzzle. Humans are also part of this puzzle, and we are far from understanding it. If nature was a clock upon which we depended, and we were taking it apart, it would be foolish to throw any parts away before we found out how it worked.

We need the earth's other living things. We use some in obvious ways, for food and medicine. We depend on others, too, sometimes in ways we do not yet understand. By hastening the extinction of thousands of organisms, humans may endanger their own future.

The earth has never before seen a species like ours. No other species has had such damaging effects on the earth's atmosphere, water, soils, and life. We may yet change our envi-

ronment so that we all die out. Humans can become extinct, too.

The idea of human extinction is not very pleasant. Humans have existed for about four million years so far, a short time compared with the dinosaurs or cockroaches. In the long view of the earth's history, however, the death of a species is no more remarkable than the death of one rabbit. Both are natural. Other living things survive, and change. The earth's elements flow on, from one living thing to another. There is beauty, variety, and change, and death helps make it all possible.

# Glossary

ALBINO An animal that lacks its normal color. Albino mammals usually have white hair or fur, and pink eyes.

ATMOSPHERE An "ocean" of gases that surround some planets. The main gases of the earth's atmosphere are oxygen and nitrogen.

ATOM The smallest particle of an element (see ELEMENT).

BACTERIA One-celled microscopic organisms (usually classified as plants) that cannot make their own food. Some bacteria cause diseases; many aid the decay of dead plants and animals.

CELL The basic structural unit of all living things, except viruses. The human body is made up of trillions of cells, while such organisms as amoebas consist of a single cell. The largest cells are the yolks of bird eggs.

CREMATION The burning of a dead person or other animal.

DECAY To decompose, rot, break down chemically. The process of decay is natural, inevitable, and necessary for the recycling of the earth's elements.

DECOMPOSERS Plants and animals that feed on once-living material and cause it to break down (decay).

ELEMENT A distinct variety of matter consisting of atoms of only one kind. An element cannot be broken down by ordinary chemical or physical processes. Examples of elements are oxygen, carbon, iron, and lead.

ENVIRONMENT All of the surroundings that affect an organism, including other living things, climate, and soil.

EVOLUTION The process by which the characteristics of a population or species of organisms gradually change over a period of time.

EXTINCTION The "death" of an entire species so that it no longer exists anywhere on earth.

FERTILIZATION The act or process in which sex cells combine. An egg cell is fertilized by a sperm cell. The fertilized egg then develops into an individual organism that has characteristics of both parents.

FUNGI A group of plants lacking roots, stems, leaves, and the green coloring substance, chlorophyll. Fungi include yeasts, molds, and mushrooms. They aid the decay of dead plants and animals.

GENES Molecules or groups of molecules that are part of the sex cells (and other cells) of organisms, and that contain chemical "directions" which determine the characteristics of the individual that develops from a fertilized egg.

MOLECULE The smallest possible amount of a compound that still has the characteristics of larger amounts of that substance. For example, a molecule of water is made up of just one atom of oxygen and two of hydrogen.

OXYGEN A colorless, odorless gas that makes up 21 percent of the earth's atmosphere. It is needed by nearly all plants and animals to enable them to "burn" food for energy.

POPULATION The number of individual animals or plants of a species that live in a specific area at a specific time. For example, the number of people living in the United States in the year 2000.

PREDATOR An animal that kills other animals for food. Besides such well-known examples as wolves and tigers, such animals as robins, ladybugs, and people are also predators.

PROTOZOA One-celled microscopic organisms, usually classified as animals. Some aid the process of decay. Protozoa include amoebas, stentors, and radiolarians.

SCAVENGER An animal that feeds on the remains of dead plants or animals.

✺ Further Reading ✺

Books marked with an asterisk (*) are fairly simple; the others are more difficult.

*Bendick, Jeanne. *Why Things Change.* New York: Parents' Magazine Press, 1973.

*Brandhorst, Carl, and Sylvester, Robert. *The Tale of Whitefoot.* New York: Simon and Schuster, 1968.

Calder, Nigel. *The Life Game: Evolution and the New Biology.* New York: Viking Press, 1974.

*Earle, Olive. *Scavengers.* New York: William Morrow & Co., Inc., 1973.

Hendin, David. *Death As a Fact of Life.* New York: W.W. Norton & Company, 1973.

*Klein, Stanley. *The Final Mystery.* New York: Doubleday & Company, Inc., 1974.

Langone, John. *Death Is a Noun*. Boston: Little, Brown and Company, 1972.

*McClung, Robert. *Mice, Moose, and Men: How Their Populations Rise and Fall*. New York: William Morrow & Co., Inc., 1973.

*Pringle, Laurence. *Ecology: Science of Survival*. New York: Macmillan Publishing Company, 1971.

*Viorst, Judith. *The Tenth Good Thing About Barney*. New York: Atheneum Publishers, 1971.

*Zim, Herbert, and Bleeker, Sonia. *Life and Death*. New York: William Morrow & Co., Inc., 1970.

# Index

Boldface type indicates a photograph